THE HUNGARIAN REVOLUTION
1956

written and compiled by **Ákos Réthly**
designed and edited by **Tímea Adrián**

consultant **Eörsi László** historian

Premier Press Publishing, Budapest, 2006
Private Planet Books

private planet

THE HUNGARIAN REVOLUTION
1956

communist dictatorship in Hungary

At the end of World WarII, Hungary was on the losing side. The Paris Peace Pact reinforced the conditions of the Trianon Pact, thus annexing 72% of Hungarian territory and 64% of the Hungarian population to neighboring countries. The war left behind demolished cities and a people that suffered casualties, captivity and death. "Behind the back of the country", the victorious powers – the United States of America, Great Britain and the Soviet Union – decided that Hungary would come under the rule of the Soviets and their all-powerful leader, Stalin.

Being assured of the support of the Red Army, communist politicians within Hungary's coalition government managed to gradually strengthen their power, thereby repressing the rising democratic developments. The communists aggressively built up and placed in leading positions their clique in order to gain control over every area of life. Therefore, instead of freedom and independence, a new era of occupation and dictatorship began in Hungary, and the country's leadership was formed by a group of communist politicians who were completely loyal and brainlessly submissive to Stalin's dictatorial wishes and the Soviet Union's interests.

On the 12th of June in 1948 the two workers' parties were united under the name Hungarian Workers' Party (MDP). In reality, this fusion meant incorporating into the Communist Party the Social Democratic Party that had been previously debilitated by several illegal means. Árpád Szakasits was elected president of the new, united party, having been vested with sham authority. The actual leader was secretary general Mátyás Rákosi. Nominally, the main decision-making body was the congress, and the party was directed by the 100-110 members of the Central Leadership nominated by the congress. The Central Leadership then elected the much narrower circle of the Political Committee, which despite its small membership had the greatest sphere of influ-ence and authority. The party numbered more than a million members. In those days it was not possible to gain any type of leadership position or responsible job unless one was a member of the communist party.

By 1948-1949 the Soviet model of totalitarianism became reality in Hungary, its main characteristics being one party; state life submitted to the communist party's top leaders; mistrust and blame within the party due to the failure to produce expected economical indexes; intellectual and physical isolation of the country; forced agricultural collectivism; legal and material despoilment of the peasantry; forced industrialization; planned

economy; constant shop-shortage; cold-war hysteria; enforced worship of party leaders; state terror to keep the population in constant fear.

Fear was a part of people's lives whether they were antagonistic toward the system or not. The political police – called ÁVH and controlled by the communist party – could arrest, imprison, torture or kill anyone any time without charge or apparent reason.

Stalin died in 1953 and the new chair of the Soviet party began a "de-stalinization" process, which resulted in significant changes even in Hungary. Rákosi as lead authority was replaced by Imre Nagy who then took some important steps both in the economy and in eliminating the government's illegitimate actions. He was outrivaled by his opponents, led by Rákosi, at the end of 1954, although it was not possible for them to take control in the same way as they had done before. Nikita S. Khrushchev, the new Soviet secretary general, exposed and condemned some of Stalin's sins in his speech at the 22nd congress on the 25th of February, 1956, which further melted the political situation in Hungary as well as in Poland. After his illegitimate actions were exposed, Rákosi – with Soviet concurrence – was discharged in July, 1956. Ernő Gerő, quite similar to Rákosi, became his successor.

In June, workers in Poznań, Poland began demonstrations for better living and working conditions and demanded free elections. The revolt was ruthlessly squelched by communist authorities, with 70 casualties and 250 arrested demonstrators. Nevertheless, unrest continued to characterize the atmosphere in industrial centers.

The process of careful political pacification began with the help of some reformist leaders who had been in intra-party opposition and ousted by the leadership. However, the situation took a critical turn as Soviet troops were being sent to Warsaw, the capital, to offer armed assistance to the hard-line communist leaders. The Polish armed forces, sympathizing with the reform plans, began fortifying strategic points of the city, joined by workers and university students in a demonstrative way. The threat of intervention being very real, W. Gomulka, the repositioned reformist party leader, succeeded in convincing Khrushchev that changes in political personnel would stabilize the communist system instead of endangering it.

A few days later, on the 23rd of October, Szabad Nép, the party's daily paper publishes the speech in which the new, reform-committed Polish leadership unfolds previous mistakes and unlawfulness, evaluates Poznań demonstrations and demands, and deems them legitimate.

DEMANDS OF THE REVOLUTIONISTS
EXCERPTS FROM THE 16 POINTS OF THE STUDENTS

"–Withdraw Soviet troops! (...)
–General elections in this country, with universal suffrage, secret ballot and the participation of several Parties, a new National Assembly and the right to strike for the workers!
–The re-examination of all political and economic trials by independent courts and the release and rehabilitation of innocent persons! The immediate repatriation of prisoners-of-war deported to the USSR.
–Complete freedom of opinion and expression, freedom of the press and a free Radio! (...)
–Stalin's statue should be removed! (...)
–Introduction of a new, national coat of arms!"

October 23, Tuesday

■ Szabad Nép, the daily newspaper of the communist party, in an article titled "New Spring Muster", welcomes the demonstrations scheduled for the evening. The event is organized by university youth sympathizing with the Polish workers.

■ The government delegation comes home from talks in Yugoslavia with party leader Ernő Gerő. To solve the crisis, they immediately go to the Party Headquarters in Akadémia Street to join the meeting of the Hungarian Workers' Party's (MDP) Political Committee.

■ 12:53 Radio Kossuth, the state radio station, interrupts its broadcast and announces the bulletin in which the Department of the Interior bans the demonstration.

■ During the course of the day more and more official and non-official organizations declare their intention to join the demonstration. The students mobilize factory workers. Authorities order military reinforcements to protect the building of the Hungarian Radio and other strategic institutions.

■ 14:23 Radio Kossuth interrupts its broadcast again to announce the decision of the Department of the Interior to give permission for the demonstration, since authorities had reevaluated the situation and deemed it less risky.

■ 15:00 A demonstration in sympathy with the Polish people begins at Petőfi's statue on Március 15. Square. In the presence of university students and professors, a student reads the sixteen demands that were approved at the student conference held at the Technical University the day before. The crowd of ten thousand begins its walk to Bem Square.

■ Technical University students and professors are gathering at Bem's statue, soon to be joined by factory workers, military officers and members of the intelligentsia. Many cut out the Soviet-inspired coat of arms from the Hungarian flag, creating a hole in the middle.

The flag with a hole that is seen here for the first time later becomes the symbol of the revolution. Following a few speeches, the crowd, now grown to fifty thousand, starts on its way towards the Houses of Parliament to hear Imre Nagy, who had been previously ousted by the hard-line communists, but is now restored into a lower position. The crowd is closely lined up, remains orderly and has a cheerful attitude, even though more and more chant radical slogans like: "Russians, go home!"; "If you are Hungarian, you are with us!"; "Imre Nagy to government, Rákosi to riverbed!"

■ 17:00 The first groups arrive at the Houses of Parliament on Kossuth Square. Within an hour the whole square and the surrounding streets fill up with people now counting two hundred thousand. Street-lighting is turned off at 6:30, but the people remain. By the light of burning newspapers the crowd is calling for Imre Nagy. The lights are turned back on. At around 6 o'clock a bigger group separates itself from the crowd and sets out to Stalin's statue on Dózsa György Street.

■ At the same time, a group of students marches to the Hungarian Radio to have their 16-point list of demands read off. The leadership of the radio denies their request. The students try to push themselves in the building, but the firm resistance of military protecting the building makes them back off.

■ 20:00 Radio Kossuth broadcasts Ernő Gerő's declaration. He talks about a chauvinistic, nationalistic and anti-Semite revolt, and promises bleak prospects and retorsion to the participants.

■ After 8 o'clock the atmosphere at the radio is becoming more and more charged, until the growing crowd breaks in. The guards, with the assistance of armed soldiers and heavy weaponry, at this point are able to force the besiegers back without shooting.

■ 21:00 After hours of hesitation and in response to the pleading of party leadership, Imre Nagy appears on the balcony of the Houses of Parliament. His addressing the crowd with the word "comrades" creates a general disappointment, and so does his promise to continue the reforms begun in 1953. Upon finishing his speech, Nagy leaves the scene to join the party's leadership meeting. The crowd breaks up.

■ 21:37 The crowd demolishes Stalin's statue, the pedestal bare of its statue with the pair of boots on it soon to become a long-term symbol of the revolution, as well as the target of budapesters' jokes.

■ 22:00 At about this time, following some futile attempts to dismiss the crowd, troops at the Radio shoot at the demonstrators. The news "young people are being killed at the Radio" quickly spreads throughout the city. Many set out to pick up guns and ammunition at local barracks and armories, while others grab weapons from the military units at the Radio. With guns in their hands, the peaceful demonstrators now turn into revolters. The majority being factory laborers and trainees, their actions are far from being politically deliberate. They have one common goal, though: to fight for their country's independence and for the overthrow of the government.

■ 22:00 The crowd besieges the headquarters of Szabad Nép daily paper. Fights begin at several other key locations: at telephone centrals, armories and presses.

■ 23:00 MDP's Central Leadership co-opts some previously excluded reformers. The meeting goes on until dawn. With some hard-line party leaders present, they form a Military Committee in order to put down the conflict with the assistance of forces devoted to the government and the Soviet Army.

■ Late at night, Soviet party leadership in Moscow – having consulted with Hungarian communist leaders – makes the decision to commit the Red Army and put down the revolution.

October 24, Wednesday

■ The first Soviet corps, comprising 6,000 servicemen, armored cars, cannons and 290 land-cruisers, arrives in Budapest between 2 and 4 a.m. Their original intent is to openly demonstrate their power, but to their surprise, they encounter armed resistance at several locations. The revolutionaries are involved in shootouts with Hungarian military and police loyal to the government at armories and police stations, while attacking the Soviet convoys.

■ The siege of the Radio ends at dawn with the victory of the revolters, leaving many victims on both sides.

■ Soviet Deputy Prime Minister Mikoyan, Central Committee member Suslov and head of Politburo (KGB) Serov arrive in Budapest, sent by Soviet party leadership for information, contact and assertion of Soviet interest. Talks are carried on first in the Ministry of Defense, and later in the party headquarters.

■ 4:30 The official radio – its studio having been moved to the Houses of Parliament – continues to broadcast the government's announcement: "Fascist, reactionary groups have made a counter-revolutionary attack against the state."

■ 8:13 The radio announces that the Central Committee had confirmed Gerő in his position, and Imre Nagy had been appointed Prime Minister, as well as elected into the Party Committee. Some of Nagy's supporters also gain important positions.

■ 8:45 Martial Law is announced with the signature of the Prime Minister in order to preserve peace and order. Curfew and the ban of assembly are also decreed. Schools and offices are closed, people don't go to work. The announcement of Martial Law is repeated several times.

CONTEMPORARY JOKES ON STALIN'S DEMOLISHED STATUE

– Who is the most eager for Santa to come?
– Stalin, he left his boots out in October.

–What should take the place of Stalin's statue?
– A fountain, so that those who have been licking his boots now could rinse their mouths.

– When will Stalin's statue be audible for the first time?
– When a bell is founded from it.

STALIN'S STATUE

A decree was issued in 1949 to raise a statue in Budapest of Stalin, the greatest living communist leader. There was a closed competition where 25 designs were submitted – some better, some purposefully worse. Sculptor Sándor Mikus was favored with the order. His 8-meter high statue weighing 65 quintals was inaugurated December 16, 1951 on Felvonulási Square that was built at the same time. This square was the regular scene of the communists' huge public events, parades and musters, where tens and hundreds of thousands of workers would be ordered to "voluntarily" and "enthusiastically" celebrate their party leaders who would wave to them from the tribune raised on the pedestal of Stalin's statue.

▦ 12:00 Imre Nagy gives a speech from the radio studio set up in the Houses of Parliament, admonishing the people to end the fight, at the same time promising to carry out the reforms previously decided but never actually begun.

▦ 12:00 Revolters occupy Athenaeum Press, where they begin the uncensored production of fly-sheets and topical printed materials.

▦ The first armed, resistant units are formed in the afternoon by groups of laborers, students, professionals and youth, some of them to become efficient brigades later. Significant groups are being formed at Baross Square, Práter Street and Corvin Alley in Pest, and Széna Square in Buda. The most intense clashes between the Soviet troops and the fighters of the 8th and 9th district – namely Corvin Alley, Práter, Tűzoltó and Tompa Street – take place at the intersection of Nagykörút and Üllői Street and at the Kilián Armory.

▦ While several rural towns start demonstrations similar to those in Budapest, most of the villages remain quiet. In the countryside, the revolution brings mainly administrative changes: the dissolution of kolkhozes, the formation of laborers' councils, the re-formation of local bodies of former democratic parties banned under Rákosi, and the discharge of old party, state or economic leaders.

IMRE NAGY 1896–1958

He was taken prisoner-of war on the Russian front in WWI, where he became familiar with communistic ideas.

He took on different roles in politics first in the Soviet Union, and after 1945 in Hungary. From 1944 he held high party and state offices. Between June 1953 and April 1955, while he was Prime Minister, he fought out some significant changes. While Rákosi and Gerő were presidents he belonged to the opposition and became the role model for the supporters of the reform and an emblematic figure of renewal. As Prime Minister during the revolution he gradually identified himself with the crowd's demands. His popularity was unanimous

page 20 >

October 25, Thursday

■ The authorities are preparing for a counter-stroke directed by the Military Committee.

■ 5:38 The Radio broadcasts the announcement of the party's Budapest Committee, in which they charge all workers to go to work. The school-break is still in effect.

■ 6:23 The bulletin of the Secretary Council is broadcast on the Radio, in which they declare as a fact that "the counter-revolutionary coup-attempt has been repressed". In the morning, government authorities reclaim the building of the Radio with the assistance of Soviet troops.

■ Demonstrations begin in the morning at several locations of the capital: on Deák Square, Bartók Béla Street and at the Hotel Astoria. Demonstrators from all directions set out to the Houses of Parliament at Kossuth Square, where they demand the appearance of Imre Nagy and the resignation of Ernő Gerő. Meanwhile, Soviet soldiers on duty at the defense of the Parliament begin to make friends with the demonstrators, many of whom even climb the tanks (with peaceful intentions).

■ 11:15 Shots are coming out of buildings on Kossuth Square, soon to be returned by tanks outside. Soviet tankers outside Kossuth Square, believing that their comrades are being ambushed, ruthlessly fire back at the crowd. It is still unclear whether the tragedy, leaving 70 to 80 people dead and 100 to 150 injured, was due to a calculated provocation or simple chaos and panic. However, the public holds the ÁVH responsible for the massacre.

■ In the course of the morning, the party's leadership – having consulted with the Soviets – makes some personnel decisions. Realizing there is little chance for immediate pacification, they initiate some real changes with actual political effect. Discharging Gerő, they elect János Kádár as first secretary of the party.

when he declared the establishment of the multi-party system, Hungary's neutrality and the withdrawal from the Warsaw Pact. Following the defeat he sought asylum at the Yugoslav Embassy. From there he was deported to Romania, then arrested and prosecuted. He declined to resign as Prime Minister and would not acknowledge the Kádár cabinet.

He was found guilty by the court for attempting to demolish the people's democratic state and for the charge of treason, and – with the party leadership's consent – was sentenced to death. He did not plead for mercy. The judgment was executed the following day, 16 June, 1958.

One of the highlights of political changes in Hungary was his funeral on June 16th, 1989. Hundreds of thousands came to this event where – along with fellow martyrs – he was reburied during a memorial service worthy of him. He was freed from all charges that had been made against him and was rehabilitated.

■ 15:00 Kádár and Nagy, the two most popular and still authentic politicians, give a speech on the radio. Kádár calls the demonstrators sincere and good-willed, noting that some counter-revolutionary forces have insinuated themselves into the crowd. Nagy promises reforms and brings up the possibility of the evacuation of Soviet troops.

■ New Soviet corps – another three divisions comprising 20,000 soldiers – arrives to Budapest from Romania and the Soviet Union. Fierce fighting starts again at several locations in the afternoon. Colonel Pál Maléter, Director of Duty at the Military Ministry, is assigned to defend the Kilián Armory. He negotiates a ceasefire with the revolters. Later, joined by his army men, he takes sides with the revolution.

October 26, Friday

■ In the morning, MDP's central leadership is considering a political solution, but no actual steps are taken. Members of the Military Committee, however, hasten an armed repression of the revolt.

■ By the afternoon, party leadership, on condition that revolters stop fighting, holds out a promise of a new, national government, talks with the Soviets on independence and equality as well as other changes. However, groups of revolters are further strengthened even in suburban areas. The Soviets suffer significant losses throughout the capital.

■ In the countryside demonstrations against Rákosi and armed fights against authorities are rising. Crowds are being shot at in the cities of Mosonmagyaróvár, Kecskemét and Miskolc. Many unarmed civilians are killed.

■ Military leadership initiates a powerful artillery attack to mop up revolutionary units at Corvin Alley. Knowing that a great number of civilian victims could be expected in this area of high inhabitancy, Imre Nagy does not authorize the attack.

THE MOLOTOV-COCKTAIL

One of the simplest and best offensive weapons against tanks in city guerilla warfare is the Molotov-cocktail. It was named after Molotov, one of Stalin's intimates. The classic version of the Molotov-cocktail was used for the first time in 1939-40 by the Finns when they were fighting off the attack of the Red Army. It became famous through the 1956 Hungarian revolution when it was commonly used against Soviet tanks.

page 24 >

October 27, Saturday

■ A new, quasi-coalitional government is formed in the morning, with personnel deemed trustworthy by Soviet advisers. Even politicians from the former Smallholders' Party are granted ministries, although not in order to represent their former party; it is their personal prestige that grants them a position. Even so, the set-up of the new government causes disappointment amongst the freedom fighters, since some new cabinet members are known as the party's old loyalists. At the same time, young, independent politicians who are committed to the reform are not on the list.

■ János Kádár and Imre Nagy suggest during talks with the Soviet delegates that Soviet tanks should leave the city to ensure the ceasefire.

■ Hard-line members of the Military Committee that was formed earlier turn against moderate party leaders and the coalitional government, thus hindering the authorities and the revolutionaries from coming to an agreement.

■ Groups of revolters besiege and occupy several police stations and party buildings, ravaging many. They throw to the streets and burn communist symbols and books containing communistic ideology.

■ At about 19:00 a new plan to defeat the armed group at Corvin Alley is developed, figuring on a joint effort of Soviet and Hungarian armed forces.

■ American Secretary of State J. F. Dulles gives a public message in his Dallas address. He declares that the United States of America does not consider Hungary its ally, meaning that they will not interfere in its affairs. He reminds the Soviet leadership of that fact two days later.

The Budapest formula for a Molotov-cocktail is a bottle filled with gasoline fitted with a gasoline-saturated rag. When it is set on fire and thrown at an object the flaming gasoline breaking out of the bottle can set even the smallest nook on fire. Many tanks and armored vehicles were disabled with Molotov-cocktails in Budapest.

October 28, Sunday

■ In the morning, Soviet and Hungarian forces begin a poorly planned action against Corvin Alley. The revolutionaries beat off the attack, destroying several tanks. Fights are also fierce in Széna Square, where soldiers manage to temporarily drive revolutionists away.

■ Leadership of MDP redefines events, calling them national democratic changes. The state party also goes through a significant alteration, János Kádár positioned as leader of the six-member chair. They declare the leading role of the communist party, the preservation of the people's democratic state and Hungary's membership with the Eastern bloc countries in the Warsaw Pact.

■ 13:20 To consolidate the situation, Imre Nagy declares a truce. A political solution seems feasible.

■ 17:25 In his radio address, Imre Nagy calls the events a "national democratic movement", with independence and a democratic political system at its focus. He announces the agreement to evacuate Soviet corps, and promises the upcoming dissolution of ÁVH.

■ Revolutionary Committees are being formed throughout the country, taking control over towns and villages. Laborers' councils set out to autonomously direct factories and labor-organizations.

■ 23:25 The formation of the vigilance organization, the National Guard, is announced. They expect students and workers to volunteer.

■ UN Security Council puts "the Hungarian question" on its agenda, with the Soviets voting against it. The Hungarian delegate opposes the decision. In his evaluation of the events, the Soviet ambassador speaks of "a fascist revolt of a small number of counter-revolutionists". A more detailed examination of the issue is postponed at the request of the Soviet delegation.

Oktober 29, Monday

■ During the night former hard-line party leaders and their families escape on an airplane to Moscow, with the help of the Soviets.

■ Representatives of 8th and 9th district revolters continue negotiations with political, military and police authorities. The fact that revolters do not have a united captaincy or a leadership that is supported and followed by each individual brigade, is a great hindrance to these talks. The variety of demands coming from different armed groups further impedes the negotiations.

■ In spite of the government's intentions toward consolidation, clashes continue throughout the city during the day. The changes that have been declared ensure revolutionists of their success, power and victory, however they feel that the promises fall short regarding their ultimate goal: multi-party elections and the withdrawal of Soviet troops. They are determined to fight until they reach those goals.

■ The supreme legislature (the government) moves from the party headquarters to the Houses of Parliament, signifying the fact that the power has been shifted from the state party to the government.

■ Evacuation of Soviet corps begins in the evening.

■ The Suez Crisis breaks out when Israel, Great Britain and France attack Egypt. This conflict diverts the world's attention from the Hungarian revolution.

THE SUEZ CRISIS

The President of Egypt announced in the summer of 1956 that the Suez Canal that had been controlled by the English and the French would come under Egyptian control and belong to the State. Great Britain and France determined to take military action in order to regain control over this strategic waterway. Upon forming an alliance with Israel, they attacked Egypt on the 29th of October. Thus the Hungarian revolution and the Suez crisis were on the UN's agenda simultaneously. Both the Soviet Union and the USA objected to the British and French action.

October 30, Tuesday

■ A smaller coalitional body called Government Cabinet is formed. Its members are politicians who are favorably judged by the public.

■ The government acknowledges the new autonomous authorities and the Revolutionary Workers' Councils. Based on the decree of Ferenc Münnich, Minister of the Interior, they proclaim the dissolution of the ÁVH.

■ József Dudás, one of the most controversial figures of the revolution, launches a new, anti-government newspaper called Independence. He occupied the headquarters of Szabad Nép the previous day with his armed men. Later he will be in negotiations with Imre Nagy who criticizes him for giving the impression to other countries that the revolution lacks unity. With no one to partner with him, he is soon to become isolated.

■ Revolters attack the Köztársaság Square headquarters of the Budapest Party Committee, where loyal political and armed forces hold one of their bases. Apart from party functionaries, the building is protected by ordered regulars of the ÁVH. The siege goes on for hours until the military tanks ordered to the scene settle the fight: they mistakenly join in on the side of the revolutionaries. Upon the occupation of the building twenty of the capitulated, disarmed defenders are lynched as an expression of general hatred towards the ÁVH. The mass hysteria does not die down even after the siege: using excavators, people are digging huge holes in the ground, hoping to find secret torture chambers and prisons that according to hearsay are set up underground.

■ 14:30 Imre Nagy officially declares the abolishment of the single-party system and the preparations for free elections.

■ In the party leadership's debate in Moscow, Khrushchev urges further de-stalinization, thus forcing the hard-liners into the defensive. Chances of a peaceful solution are growing.

October 31, Wednesday

- The supreme authority of the Hungarian Catholic Church, Cardinal József Mindszenty is released from his house-arrest. He was sentenced for life and imprisoned in 1949 based on concocted charges by the communists.

- In the morning, revolters, military and members of the police form the Committee of Revolutionary Forces in the Kilián Barracks under the direction of Béla Király (Commander-in-Chief of the National Guard and Budapest) and Colonel Sándor Kopácsi (Superintendent of the Budapest Police). This armed body is formed to restore order, prevent provocations, create the conditions of consolidation, and to integrate freedom fighters' brigades into the National Guard.

- The party MDP's leadership announces its dissolution, and at the same time forms a new party under the name Hungarian Socialist Workers' Party (MSZMP).

- Previously banned democratic parties are being reorganized and re-activated one by one. Several new, revolutionary parties are also established.

- In Moscow, at a Central Committee meeting of the Soviet Communist Party, hard-liners who urge armed intervention in Hungary prevail over Khrushchev, which is to be attributed to his hesitancy after failure in handling the Suez crisis and his fear of losing even more power. They think that any permissiveness on their part may reflect the weakness of the Soviet Union and the communist movement. They also fear that the Hungarian fight for freedom might spread to other socialist countries. Thus, they decide to intervene and also to assist in the positioning of leadership that would be carefully selected by them. The responsibility to plan the operations under the cover-name "Whirlwind" is entrusted to Marshall Zukov, Secretary of Defence. The mission is to be led by Marshall Konev, Commander-in Chief of the United Armed Forces of the Warsaw Pact.

November 1, Thursday

■ Soviet operations are launched throughout the country in the morning. Airports are closed down and further Soviet columns enter the country from the East. Imre Nagy orders in Soviet Ambassador Uri Andropov who gives an elusive reply when asked about the operations.

■ In response to the Soviet intervention the government declares Hungary's military neutrality and withdrawal from the Warsaw Pact (the military alliance of communist countries), initiates negotiations with the Soviet Union, and appeals to the Great Powers to guarantee Hungary's neutrality. With this declaration, the legal basis for Soviet military action is removed, thus granting the freedom fighters' supreme demand. The declaration significantly raises Nagy's and the government's support.

■ Late at night János Kádár and Minister of the Interior Ferenc Münnich secretly go to the Soviet Embassy to clarify the situation. They end up leaving the country via the Tököl Soviet military base escorted by the Soviets. They leave their colleagues, their confidantes and their families without notice.

■ 22:00 In his radio address, János Kádár praises the revolution, announces the formation of the new party, MSZMP, and declares its intention to break away from all political errors made in the past.

November 2, Friday

■ In the morning, the government delegates representatives to negotiations on the withdrawal from the Warsaw Pact, on the withdrawal of the Soviet troops and to the UN meeting respectively.

■ Imre Nagy protests several times at the Soviet Embassy against the influx of the Soviet army and the enclavement of Budapest. He informs other countries' ambassadors of Soviet operations.

■ The Captaincy of the National Guard develops its plan to defend Budapest.

■ János Kádár and Ferenc Münnich attend the meeting of the Soviet Communist Party's Central Committee. While Kádár gives an accurate description of the situation and suggests a political solution, Münnich urges military intervention.

■ Key defense points in Budapest are being fortified with heavy artillery.

■ Soviet party leaders meet with Yugoslav president Tito, who is not against suppressing the revolution. He thinks that instead of Münnich, Kádár should be appointed Prime Minister. Khrushchev gives his consent. Apart from the immediate allies of the Soviet Union, even China urges military intervention.

JÁNOS KÁDÁR 1912–1989

He joined the leftist movement in 1931. He was gradually placed into higher positions following WWII. As Minister of the Interior it was his responsibility to organize and direct liquidations and fabricated trials as well as other illegal actions. During the 1956 revolution he was considered a popular reform-politician and like Imre Nagy, belonged to the leading state and party bodies supporting the revolt. On November 1st he secretly traveled to Moscow to seek a peaceful solution. It took only a few days for the Soviet party leadership to convince him to go over to their side. From that time on he was Hungary's

page 38 >

November 3, Saturday

■ Imre Nagy's cabinet turns into a coalition when prominent leaders from communist, social democratic, smallholders' and other parties join in. Pál Maléter is appointed Secretary of Defense. Kádár is appointed member of the government in his absence.

■ 10:00 Negotiations with the Soviets are begun over details of their military withdrawal and the importance of protecting Soviet monuments in the country. At the same time, new military movements are started throughout Hungary: Soviets close the Western border next to Austria. In the East by the Soviet Union, they occupy key railway and highway junctions and border stations.

■ 20:00 In a radio address, Cardinal Mindszenty declares the main goals being the restoration of democracy and the establishment of justice and equality. He urges the returning of Christian institutions that had been socialized or eliminated by the communist system.

■ 21:00 Hard-liners at the Moscow party meeting propose that Münnich should be the new Prime Minister, but Khrushchev is already supporting Kádár. His effective reasoning about Kádár being the easier to control convinces the rest of the Committee. Thus Kádár is given the position.

■ 22:00 Negotiations on Soviet withdrawal are going on at the Tököl Army Base. In the first few minutes General Serov, ex-director of Soviet secret police KGB, enters the scene and arrests the Hungarian delegation headed by Secretary of Defense Pál Maléter.

supreme political leader for 33 years, always considering Soviet interests. His era was a so-called "soft dictatorship", hence the sarcastic nickname for Hungary: "the happiest barrack".

Following the changes in international politics that also reached Hungary, Kádár was dismissed from all of his positions at the end of the eighties. He died after a long illness on July 6th, 1989, in the same hour when Imre Nagy was rehabilitated.

November 4, Sunday

■ Further Soviet troops arrive in Hungary during the night.

■ 4:00 An overall Soviet action begins. The country's borders are closed down, railway junctions and other strategic locations are occupied and the disarmament of the Hungarian army begins.

■ 5:05 The Ungvár (Uzhorod) Radio in the Soviet Union broadcasts "an open letter to the Hungarian people", announcing the formation of the Revolutionary Workers' and Peasants' Government and János Kádár as its Prime Minister. Most of the cabinet members are informed about their membership through the radio.

■ 5:20 Imre Nagy gives a dramatic radio speech on the Soviet attack and the situation of the cabinet both in Hungarian and in several world languages. The recording of this proclamation is repeated several times.

■ After 6:00 Imre Nagy, his immediate colleagues, several members of the cabinet and their families seek and are granted asylum at the Yugoslav Embassy. Cardinal Mindszenty seeks asylum at the US Embassy

■ István Bibó is the only cabinet member still in the Parliament building. He issues a manifesto in which he identifies himself with the revolution, appealing to the Great Powers of the world to stand by Hungary on the basis of the UN's Constitution.

■ It's mostly young people who continue putting up a stout resistance. There are fights both in the inner city and in the suburbs of Budapest. Hoping that the West and the UN will soon come to their aid, freedom fighters do their best to persevere. Although in a couple of districts they do inflict heavy losses on the invaders, those, superior in numbers, destroy their power of resistance by the weekend. Soviets take overall control and set up military government of occupied territory. The arrests of revolters and leaders of the revolution begin.

defeat and retaliation

Even though the routing of armed groups is finished by the 10th-11th of November, political resistance endures until the spring of 1957.

The revolution and the fight for freedom ended with a significant number of casualties. Several thousand were killed, more than half of them under 25. During the retaliation following the defeat more than twenty-two thousand were imprisoned for participating in the revolution and 229 received a death penalty. Among the executed were Prime Minister Imre Nagy, Secretary of Defense Pál Maléter and several other politicians who had taken sides with the revolution. Some two hundred thousand people left all their possessions behind and escaped from the country. Those that remained suffered harassment from the police for years or even decades to come. Those publicly sympathizing with the revolt or those that participated even to the smallest extent were not allowed to continue their studies or were forced to leave their jobs. The expression "politically unreliable" was written on their record sheet that went with them everywhere and inhibited both their professional and existential advancement. Despite its defeat the 1956 Hungarian revolution and fight for freedom remains a significant landmark in the history of Hungary and the whole communist bloc. It made the majority of Hungarians realize the fact that they could not rely on the help of Western countries to establish democracy. For the Soviet leadership it also carried a lesson: they understood that in order to maintain the stability of the Eastern bloc they needed to grant Hungary greater independence.

To the world, the Hungarian revolution and its ruthless drenching in blood was the first crack on the "unshakeable" building of communism, and also unmasked the false "People's State" image. Although the Soviet Army drenched the Hungarian fight for independence in blood, the 1956 revolt demoralized the international communist movement and was one of the landmarks that led to the collapse of the Berlin Wall, communism and the Soviet Union years later.

The Blood of the Hungarians

Albert Camus, October 23, 1957, Paris

I am not one of those who wish to see the people of Hungary take up arms again in a rising certain to be crushed, under the eyes of the nations of the world, who would spare them neither applause nor pious tears, but who then would go back to their slippers by the fireside like a football crowd on a Sunday evening after a cup final.

There are already too many dead on the field, and we cannot be generous with any but our own blood. The blood of Hungary has re-emerged too precious to Europe and to freedom for us not to be jealous of it to the last drop.

(...)

Hungary conquered and in chains has done more for freedom and justice than any people for twenty years. But for this lesson to get through and convince those in the West who shut their eyes and ears, it was necessary, and it can be no comfort to us, for the people of Hungary to shed so much blood which is already drying in our memories.

In Europe's isolation today, we have only one way of being true to Hungary, and that is never to betray, among ourselves and everywhere, what the Hungarian heroes died for, never to condone, among ourselves and everywhere, even indirectly, those who killed them.

It would indeed be difficult for us to be worthy of such sacrifices. But we can try to be so, in uniting Europe at last, in forgetting our quarrels, in correcting our own errors, in increasing our creativeness, and our solidarity. We have faith that there is on the march in the world, parallel with the forces of oppression and death which are darkening our history, a force of conviction and life, an immense movement of emancipation which is culture and which is born of freedom to create and of freedom to work.

Those Hungarian workers and intellectuals, beside whom we stand today with such impotent sorrow, understood this and have made us the better understand it. That is why, if their distress is ours, their hope is ours also. In spite of their misery, their chains, their exile, they have left us a glorious heritage which we must deserve: freedom, which they did not win, but which in one single day they gave back to us.

(Details)

blood in the water
a postlude in Melbourne

The XVI Olympic Games in Melbourne, Australia started a month after the revolution. Since Hungary was considered one of the world's sport powers and rated very well among the countries, the Hungarian delegates normally received a lot of attention. At the previous Olympic Games four years earlier, Hungary – with its 16 gold medals – ended up third on the medal chart, preceded only by the Soviet Union and the USA.

In the fall of 1956 it was not just its success in sports but also its political situation that put Hungary in the spotlight at the Olympics. Australia as hosting country and other Western countries all sympathized with the Hungarians, who, like a modern David, were brave enough to confront the Goliath of the oppressive Soviet Union.

In spite of all the difficulties in their training, travel and the controversial news received from home, Hungarian athletes gained one victory after another. They already had nine gold, ten silver and seven bronze medals when December 6, the thrilling day of the water-polo semi-final with the Soviet

Union, arrived. In the swimming stadium (that was able to hold six thousand) eight thousand fans were crammed, almost all of them cheering in concert for the Hungarian team. They obviously had the advantage: they scored four goals while the Soviets scored none. The crowd was elated, frantically cheering the victory. Water-polo matches are often tough and fouls are not uncommon. To revenge one such dubious action on the part of the Hungarian team, one of the Soviet players hit Hungarian Ervin Zádor with his elbow, fissuring the skin above his eye. Blood was rolling down his cheeks as he climbed out of the water – this time not at the locker rooms' side as normal, but facing the audience. This way he had to walk down in front of the roaring crowd that now had no reason to contain itself, breaking loose just a couple of minutes before the end of the match. Fans were jumping through the rails to take revenge on the Russians for the supposed atrocity.

Under the given circumstances it was impossible to continue the match, so it ended with the Hungarian teams' 4:0 victory. The police had to come to the Soviet team's rescue and take them out of the stadium. It took some effort to reestablish order. Photos of bleeding Zádor circled round the world press the following day.

not liberated but loosened

In the cold war era of the 1950's one of the main aims of the West was undermining the political system in communist countries and reducing the Soviet Union's international influence.

Radio stations like Voice of America and Radio Free Europe were founded and sponsored by US intelligence in the early 1950's. Their Hungarian language broadcasts were mainly anti-communist propaganda, disclosing the deficiencies of socialism, of the party elite and of the communist bloc. They aimed at shaking people's faith in the communist ideal, in their leaders and in the domestic media, and at destroying the media by questioning its authenticity. They hoped that the general discontent that they helped fan would trigger political resistance, as well as anti-government combinations and social actions.

Communist authorities banned listening to these radio stations, and punished offenders with administrative sanctions or even imprisonment. They had a huge apparatus to jam the broadcasts.

During the 1956 revolution these radio stations did not only keep track of the events, but also tried to influence them. They gave specific tactical advice to the fighters and encouraged them to hold on.

To the West, the Hungarian revolution came as a surprise, and despite their earlier communication, they remained passive when it was time to act. They realized in a short time that there was no chance for them either to support the revolt, or to intervene, or to provide military assistance. The so-called Yalta world order after WWII that allocated political, military and economical spheres to the Great Powers did not make any intervention possible in the split continent, Europe.

However, they failed to communicate that fact to the above-mentioned radio stations, so their broadcasts – in the accustomed manner – continued to assure listeners that NATO and the US Army would come to the aid of the revolution in a matter of days.

The aid never arrived, and Western passivity made it clear that Soviet occupation was to be considered long-term and any fight against it should be placed on a different platform. Thus, the tactic of "loosening up the ideology" took the place of the earlier "liberation strategy". The two radio stations became the means of this new strategy in the following years, after they managed to regain their authenticity lost during the revolution.

behind the iron curtain

The intervention of the Soviet Army was legitimated by the so-called Revolutionary Workers' and Peasants' Government. János Kádár became the country's main leader with the consent of Soviet party leadership. It was more and more obvious that independence and democracy, being the basic goals of the revolt would not become a reality. It was also clear that Stalinist politics that characterized the years before 1956 were gone for good. The stabilization period until the beginning of the 1960's was characterized first by retaliation against the revolutionists, then by the restoration of dictatorial institutions and stabilizing Kádár's personal power, and finally by gaining international recognition for the country.

Kádár's willingness to compromise and his famous motto "Whoever is not against us is with us!" created a broad social consensus in the population that wanted peace and personal welfare. However, this liberalization was still limited: a communistic single-party system, absolute loyalty to the Soviet Union's foreign policy and to the Warsaw Pact had to remain, as well as accepting the definition of the 1956 revolution as a "fascist, revisionist counter-revolution".

The domestic situation in Hungary gradually grew milder from the 1960's. It was the era of the "soft dictatorship". From 1968 on, the control over planned economy began to loosen up mainly out of economic necessity. Soviet foreign policy also softened up to some extent. Some reform-communists within the party realized the need for change, but they envisioned nothing more than a careful and controlled loosening up. In the middle of the 1980's some swift changes took place internationally: the newly elected secretary of the Soviet Communist Party, Mikhail Gorbachev, realized that his country, as well as the whole communist system, had reached an economic and political crisis, so it would be impossible to maintain the power zone of Central-Eastern Europe.

Following the changes in foreign politics, underground circles that had been active in Hungary for years began formulating parties and strived for greater publicity and a role in politics. Parliament issued the right to form parties in 1989, and MSZMP (the only existing party up to the moment) recognized the legality of the multi-party system.

One of the central events – taking place after more than thirty years – in the process of democratic changes in Hungary relates to the 1956 revolution. Imre Pozsgay, a reform-committed leader

of the communist party caused great excitement when he – after 33 years – called the 1956 events a revolt instead of a counter-revolution. Following that announcement the democratic opposition demanded a worthy memorial service and re-burial for Imre Nagy and his fellow martyrs. Their request was granted on 16th June, 1989. It was a landmark that ensured that the political changes should and could not be reverted.

Restrictions having been significantly loosened up by the end of the 1980's, almost everybody was allowed to travel to Western countries, which, near the Austrian border of Hungary, was followed by an inflow of refugees coming from East-Germany. The Hungarian government that was still expecting to remain in power, decided not to "interfere with German domestic affairs" – even at the definite request of the East-German communist leadership – and did not hinder any foreigners traveling to the West.

19th of August, 1989 marks the day of the so-called Pan-European Picnic held on the Austrian-Hungarian border, a celebration symbolizing the rapprochement of formerly opposed countries and the opening of the border. The unexpected appearance and action of some East-German refugees breaking through the fence was met by a passive reaction on the part of the Hungarian guards, thus making the demolition of the "Iron Curtain" both realistic and inevitable. This was one event in the reform process that made the closure of Hungary and the whole Eastern Bloc useless and indefensible. The process led to the demolition of the Berlin Wall in November and the reunion of the two German states.

The political changes took place in Hungary in a peaceful way, without bloodshed. Free parliamentary elections were held in the spring of 1990 where former oppositional forces gained the majority of votes. The autocracy of the communist party was definitively over. Talks were begun on the withdrawal of the Soviet Army. Changes took place in all areas of life; even symbols such as the Soviet-inspired coat of arms were re-designed. Communist holidays were abolished, red stars were taken down throughout the country and monuments symbolizing the totalitarian system were relegated to a statue park.

Members of the Warsaw Pact signed the papers abolishing the Eastern military bloc on the 25th of February, 1991. The supreme, common goal for which so many fought and gave their lives or personal freedom became a reality after 35 years: the 19th of June, 1991 was the day when the last Soviet soldier left Hungary.

Statuepark, Budapest
gigantic monuments from the age of communist dictatorship

"The park is about dictatorship and the moment this can be spoken aloud, written down and expressed in architecture, the park will really be about democracy. Only democracy can give us a chance to think freely about dictatorship – or about democracy or anything else for that matter."

(Eleőd Ákos architect, the conceptual artist
for the Statuepark– Memento Park in Budapest, 1994)

illustration

Historical Archives of the Security Services, Budapest (ÁSZTL)

Private collections and photo-archives as indicated

Historical Photo-Archives of the Hungarian National Museum, Budapest (MNM)

Photo-Archives of the Hungarian News Agency, Budapest (MTI)

cover page

▩ "1 Boot Square" – the pedestal of toppled statue of Stalin with the boots remaining, plus the Hungarian national flag and waving revolutionists, Dózsa György Street (Parade Ground Square), October 24, 1956. Photo: Dr. Miklós Balás (MNM)

pages 2-3

▩ Reliefs on Stalin's statue (portions), Dózsa György Street (Parade Ground Square), October, 1956. Unknown photographer (ÁSZTL)

page 5

▩ Working women on a parade, Dózsa György Street (Parade Ground Square) May 1, 1952. Unknown photographer (MNM)

page 7

▩ Portraits of Rákosi and Stalin at the parade, Dózsa György Street (Parade Ground Square), May 1, 1952. Unknown photographer (MNM)

page 8

▩ Passers-by reading the 16 demands of the students, Corner of Rákóczi Street and Múzeum Boulevard, October 23, 1956. Photo: Tamás Fényes (MTI)

page 9

▩ Demonstrative march of university students in downtown, Tanács (present-day: Károly) Boulevard October 23, 1956. Photo: Tamás Fényes (MTI)

▩ Demonstrators marching toward Bem Square, Chain Bridge, October 23, 1956. Photo: Tamás Munk

page 10

▩ Demonstrators, Bem Square, October 23, 1956. Photo: Lajos Müller (MTI)

page 11

▩ Demonstrators with the torn national flag, Corner of Bem Square and Frankel Leó Street October 23, 1956. Photo: Ferenc Fehérvári (MTI)

▩ Demonstrators at the entrance of the Parliament building, Kossuth Lajos Square, October 23, 1956. Photo: Sándor Bojár (MTI)

▩ Demonstrators in front of the Parliament building, Kossuth Lajos Square, October 23, 1956. Photo: Tamás Munk (MTI)

page 12

▩ Preparations for demolishing Stalin's statue, Dózsa György Street (Parade Ground Square), October, 1956. Photo: Lajos Müller (MTI)

page 13

▩ Stalin's statue, fallen and mutilated, 7th district, Budapest, October, 1956. Unknown photographer (ÁSZTL)

▩ Head of Stalin's statue and cast down pentacle, Corner of Rákóczi Street and Nagykörút, About 25-26 October, 1956. Unknown photographer (ÁSZTL)

page 15

▩ Building of the Hungarian Radio after the siege, words saying "Free Hungarian Radio", Bródy Sándor Street, October 24, 1956. Photo: Lajos Mészáros (MNM)

page 16

▩ Parade under arms in front of Stalin's statue, Dózsa György Street (Parade Ground Square), April 4, 1953. Photo: Unknown photographer (Archives of daily paper Szabad Nép – MNM)

page 17

▩ The pedestal of the toppled statue of Stalin, Dózsa György Street (Parade Ground Square), October 24, 1956. Photo: Dr. Miklós Balás (MNM)

page 18

▩ Imre Nagy giving a radio address, Temporary studio in the Parliament building, October 28, 1956. Photo: Sándor Bojár (MTI)

page 19

▩ Demonstrators and Soviet soldiers fraternizing, Kossuth Lajos Square (Parliament), October 25, 1956. Photo: Sándor Bojár (MTI)

▩ People escaping from the fusillade, Kossuth Lajos Square (Parliament), October 25, 1956. Photo: Sándor Bojár (MTI)

▩ Victims of the fusillade Kossuth Lajos Square (Parliament), October 25, 1956. Photo: Dr. Dénes Hegedűs (MNM)

page 21

▩ Revolters on a tank, Bródy Sándor Square, October 25, 1956. Photo: Dr. László Zalay (MNM)

page 22

▩ Young girl with Molotov-cocktail, Corvin Alley, November 1, 1956. Photo: László Tóth (MNM)

resources

- "Torn from the Flag" – website of the movie, www.klaudiainc.com
- Website of The Institute for the History of the 1956 Hungarian Revolution, www.rev.hu
- Website of the American Hungarian Folklore Centrum, magyar.org
- Krónika 1956, (Chronicle 1956), Kossuth Kiadó, Tekintet Alapítvány, Budapest 2006
- Litván, György, Mítoszok és legendák 1956-ról, Évkönyv VIII. p. 205-218, 1956 Institute, Budapest 2000 (Myths and Legends About 1956, Yearbook VIII)
- Magyar Életrajzi Lexikon (1000-1990) az Interneten, Akadémiai Kiadó, Budapest, mek.oszk.hu (Online Hungarian Biographical Encyclopedia)
- Hungarian Virtual Encyclopedia, maintained by the Institute of Philosophy of the Hungarian Academy of Sciences, www.enc.hu
- Website of the Pan-European Picnic, w3.sopron.hu/paneu-piknik/
- Pótó, János, Emlékművek, politika, közgondolkodás (Monuments, Politics, Public Thinking), MTA Történettudományi Intézet, Budapest 1989
- Free online encyclopedia, www.wikipedia.hu
- Website of the Statue Park, www.szoborpark.hu
- Színes Magyarország (Colorful Hungary), Magyar Hivatalos Közlönykiadó, Budapest, 2003

Hungarian Revolution – 1956
Written and compiled by Ákos Réthly
Designed and edited by Tímea Adrián

Consultant: László Eörsi, historian

English translation by Erika J. Füstös
Technical assistant: Lőrinc Balázs

With the help of: László Alapfy, Anton Ginzburg, Zoltán György, Katalin Jalsovszky, Robert D. Kibler, Zsolt Krahulcsán, Norbert Lobenwein, Andrea Mazur, Rolf Müller, Dr. János Rumpf, Péter Szabó, Zoltán Szántó, László Szőke.
Special thanks to little Ármin and Teréz Adrián.

ISBN 963 86881 6 5

© Premier Press Kiadó (Premier Press Publishing), Budapest, 2006
Premier Press Kft., Budapest, Királyi Pál utca 10., 1053 Hungary, Private Planet Books
www.privateplanet.com